THE CHARIS LEGACY

Published by Charis Legacy Partners

www.charislegacy.com

Book design by Ivica Jandrijević

ISBN 979-8-7079982-5-6

THE CHARIS LEGACY

A Legacy Planning Guide to Maximizing Your Giving Impact

Scott Monk, CFP®, CFA, MBA

CONTENTS

PLANNING STRATEGY IN PRE-RETIREMENT YEARS (~AGES 50-65)

PLANNING STRATEGY IN RETIREMENT YEARS (~AGES 65+)

PREFACE

Many years ago, I felt a clear calling to devote my life to building wealth for the purpose of funneling as much of it as possible into the ministries and charities I felt passionately about. When I first caught this vision, I was fresh out of college, and since I came from a family of limited means, I worked and took out student loans to pay for college. All that to say, this vision came to me as I was drowning in student loan debt with no idea what this was going to look like or where it would take me. However, I decided to just step out in faith and let the vision guide me.

I carried this dream in my heart throughout business school and then through countless hours studying for the Chartered Financial Analyst® and CERTIFIED FINANCIAL PLANNER™ certifications. All the while, I would find myself daydreaming about the charitable impact I could have and spending my free time researching strategies to maximize that impact.

I wrote this book to take much of what I have learned on this journey and share it with others who carry a similar dream in their hearts. Charis (pronounced KAIR-iss) is the Greek word used in the Bible for grace, or unmerited favor, and it connotes something given freely without expectation of anything in return; it's the root word from which the English word charity is derived. The title of this book, "The Charis Legacy", encapsulates this dream of leaving a legacy of giving back, and it is my aspiration to give back to my tribe of philanthropy-minded individuals. My hope with this book and with Charis Legacy Partners is to push beyond the inherently limited charitable impact I can have on my own and broaden that impact through helping others harness their wealth to achieve their legacy goals. This book has a particular focus on charitable legacy goals, but most legacy-minded individuals want to leave a legacy for their heirs also, so I incorporate some inheritance planning as well.

I also wrote this book to serve a niche that is growing but has been grossly underserved. Along my own journey, I struggled mightily to find expert guidance to help me implement the vision I carried, so I hope to help fill that void. It also seems like the right moment in our cultural climate for content like this, when we see billionaires across the world making commitments to give away their wealth for the broader good and younger generations taking more of an interest in purposefully using their wealth to have a positive impact on society.

I have written this book for legacy-minded folks of all ages, and I have structured it in a chronological format, spanning the lifetime of a legacy builder. You are likely to find content most relevant to you in the chapter of the book that corresponds to your life stage. Having said that, there are some topics covered in each chapter that could really apply to any life stage, but to avoid duplicating content, I had to use some editorial discretion and just pick a chapter in which to feature it. I therefore suggest you at least skim each chapter to see if you find content relevant to you.

My intent was to keep this book short and sweet – with little fluff and relatively high level - and then dive deeper and draw these ideas out further in my blog, The Legacy Builder, which can be found at charislegacy.com/blog. So, if some of the content in this book piques your interest, feel free to browse the blog, as you will find there a fuller discussion of these and many other topics relevant to legacy planning.

—Scott Monk, Author

LAYING THE FOUNDATION

INTRO

My assumption in writing this book is that if you are reading it, leaving a legacy of giving back features prominently in your financial goals, which means you've already completed step one in the financial planning process[1]: determining your financial goals. It is important to remember that to create a truly lasting and sustainable legacy, you must lay the right foundation and get your own financial house in order. It's like a building: if you want it to stand over generations and not crumble with the passing of time, it must be built on a strong foundation.

---

[1] https://www.schwab.com/financial-planning-collection/8-components-of-good-financial-plan

What is a strong foundation in the context of legacy planning? Well, this takes us to step two in the financial planning process: developing a net worth statement to establish a baseline for your assets and liabilities, as well as creating a budget and doing a cash flow analysis to determine how your actual income and expenses compare to your budget. Once you have the clarity provided by this step in the financial planning process, a good financial planner can use these cash flow figures to determine how much you are likely to add to or detract from your net worth each year. He or she can then help you project into the future to determine just how much wealth you are likely to have going forward. This includes how much will be needed for spending in retirement and how much wealth over and above spending needs (known as wealth surplus) can realistically be earmarked for legacy purposes.

Taking the time to get this kind of clarity around your financial situation will reveal several important things that I will use the remainder of this chapter to expand upon.

EMERGENCY FUND

I cannot stress enough the importance of having an adequate emergency fund. One financial mishap or hardship can derail even the most grandiose legacy plans, and Murphy's Law suggests there is no escaping it – inevitably, at some point, something will go wrong. If you don't currently have an emergency fund, start with a modest goal of saving $1K in cash (preferably somewhere you can't get to it easily if temptation strikes).

Next, if you're still working, build up a cash amount equal to 3-6 months of expenses. This provides a cushion for spending shocks (like unexpected home or car repairs), but more importantly it is a cushion for income shocks; if you get laid off or otherwise lose an income stream, it buys you time to get back on your feet and find a way to replace that income.

If you're in retirement or otherwise distributing regularly from your portfolio, build up a cash position equal to at least 1-2 years of portfolio withdrawals, which insulates you from extreme market volatility. Historically, the median time for a portfolio to recover from bear market losses[2] has

---

2   https://www.barrons.com/articles/forgotten-how-to-navigate-your-retirement-portfolio-through-a-bear-market-heres-a-map-to-guide-you-51584120674

been around two years and three months. When you have a portfolio that is balanced with bonds, as most retirees do, that volatility is reduced because bonds help to counterbalance the volatility of equities, providing a buffer against the full furies of the stock market.

So, this 1-2-year cash cushion effectively insulates you from having to sell in the depths of a bear market. Without this cash cushion in your portfolio, you run the risk of exhausting your cash in the middle of a market downturn, when you could be forced to liquidate stocks while they are low.

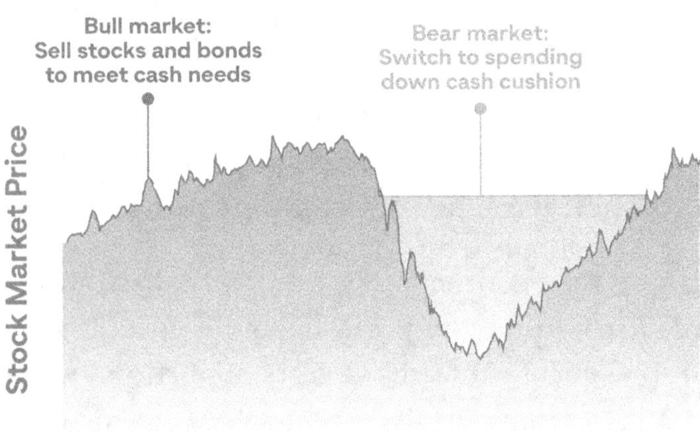

By maintaining 1–2 years of cash, the idea is that you leave that cash alone during bull markets (when the market is going up) and just sell stocks and bonds to meet your cash needs. Then, when the bull market ends and a bear market begins, you stop selling and switch to spending down your cash. By the time you've depleted that 1–2-year cash cushion, your portfolio is likely to have recovered from the worst of the bear market, so you can sell stocks and bonds again (including to replenish the cash cushion). I think of this cash as kind of like building a bridge over a steep valley, as visualized.

Finally, let's talk about options for investing this cash. In a low interest rate environment, where cash is yielding next to nothing, it can be tempting to "reach for yield"[3] by moving cash reserves into bonds or something else that pays higher interest. Keep in mind, though, that the purpose of this emergency fund is to be there when you need it unexpectedly.

Cash or money market funds are about as low-risk as you can get in the investment world (not risk-free, however, because you still have inflation risk[4]), whereas bonds carry the risk of principal

---

3 https://www.cnbc.com/2020/02/24/warren-buffett-reaching-for-yield-is-really-stupid-but-very-human.html
4 https://www.cnbc.com/2020/06/25/op-ed-there-is-no-such-thing-as-truly-risk-free-even-going-to-cash.html

losses if interest rates go up[5] (albeit much less volatile than stocks, and shorter term bonds are much less volatile than longer term bonds). So, the danger is that bonds go down in value right when you need to access that money. Because of this added risk, I generally advocate keeping emergency funds in cash or money market funds. If you are accumulating cash above and beyond the emergency fund for a short-term spending goal like a house or car purchase, where you have more clarity on the time horizon, maybe you consider short-term bonds or CDs (when you know you won't need the money until that CD matures), but you generally want to keep the emergency fund as risk-free as possible.

INSURANCE

Sticking with the subject of protecting against the risk of unexpected financial hardship, we need to talk about the role of insurance in legacy planning. Finance is all about the allocation of risk and the fair compensation for assuming that risk. In the context

---

5   https://www.fidelity.com/learning-center/investment-products/fixed-income-bonds/duration#:~:text=Generally%2C%20bonds%20with%20long%20maturities,coupons%20will%20have%20shorter%20durations.

of insurance products, you pay premiums to compensate the insurance company for assuming a risk that - were it born exclusively by you rather than distributed broadly among the insurance company's many policyholders - could prove financially ruinous to you. There are myriad types of insurance, but for the sake of brevity, I will focus here only on those I have found, based on my experience doing insurance reviews with clients, to be the most overlooked or misunderstood types of insurance.

One of the more overlooked types of insurance among young people in the accumulation stage is disability insurance[6], which replaces your income in the event of an accident or health crisis that leaves you unable to continue working in the same capacity and earning at the same level. If this happens and you didn't already have disability insurance, it's likely that any legacy plans would go out the window as you switched into financial survival mode. There are different types of disability insurance, and a good insurance broker can help you determine which one makes the most sense for you.

Life insurance is another type of insurance often taken for granted among accumulators, but life insurance is at its most valuable and cost-effective in

---

[6]   https://www.investopedia.com/terms/d/disability-insurance.asp

this stage of life[7]. In essence, life insurance protects your human capital, which is your future earnings potential. For most people early in their careers, human capital is their largest asset, because they haven't had time to accumulate financial capital. If they happen to be married or have dependents that are counting on those future earnings, life insurance fills the void left by their untimely death. Even for folks without dependents but who have legacy goals, life insurance can help ensure the legacy that would have been achieved with those future earnings.

Life insurance typically adds less value as folks get closer to the end of their careers and their human capital diminishes, replaced by actual financial assets. However, there are still some situations where it can be effective, even in retirement. For instance, if for whatever reason an older individual has not been able to accumulate much in the way of financial assets over their lifetime, but they still have strong legacy goals, upon their death, life insurance can step in for the inheritance or charitable giving they had in mind. Or, on the opposite end of the spectrum, if someone

---

7   https://www.investopedia.com/articles/investing/072816/what-best-age-get-life-insurance.asp#:~:text=Why%20Younger%20Is%20Better,you%20from%20purchasing%20a%20plan.

has accumulated significant assets over their lifetime, where they will be well into estate tax territory, they might take out a life insurance policy to cover the estate taxes, so their heirs are not stuck with the bill.

Lastly, in my many years of working with clients, I have observed that probably the most overlooked type of insurance is umbrella insurance[8], which becomes increasingly important as your net worth grows. Most people have auto and homeowners insurance, and they are probably familiar with the fact that these policies have some sort of liability coverage associated with them. For instance, if a guest gets injured on your property and decides to sue you, that liability protection kicks in and protects your assets, up to the liability coverage limit.

The problem is most of the liability coverage built into homeowners or auto insurance typically tops out at around $500K. So, what happens if, for instance, you are at fault in an auto accident with a high-income earner, such as a neurosurgeon or a professional athlete, and they sue you for loss of income and other damages because the accident

---

8   https://www.kiplinger.com/kiplinger-tools/insurance/
    t028-s002-how-much-umbrella-insurance-do-i-need/
    index.php

made them unable to work? These are the night-mare scenarios that umbrella insurance covers, because without it, this situation could bankrupt you and put to rest any dreams you had of leaving a financial legacy.

Umbrella insurance raises the liability coverage limit across all of these other policies that have built-in liability protection, up to $1 million, $5 million, or more. Ideally, you want to raise the limits to keep up with the growth of the portion of your net worth that would be exposed to creditors in a lawsuit[9]. Some assets, such as a certain portion of your qualified retirement accounts and part of the equity in your primary residence (depending on the homestead laws in your state), have built-in creditor protection. I won't go into detail on these areas, but a qualified attorney familiar with the laws in your state can provide more definitive insight into your specific situation.

So, the amount of your net worth that is exposed to creditors will dictate the level of liability protection needed. As long as your liability protection is high enough to discourage a would-be plaintiff from going to trial and instead accepting a settlement equal to or below your umbrella coverage

---

9   https://www.investopedia.com/articles/retirement/07/buildawall.asp

limit, your umbrella insurance will cover your legal fees and the settlement amount. Again, consult a qualified attorney for more detail on this aspect of umbrella insurance.

DEBT

Depending on the results of your net worth and cash flow analysis, it may turn out that you need to make paying down debt a higher priority than near-term legacy giving. Not all debt is created equal, and some debt (for instance, mortgages or student loans) can actually be useful in helping to grow your net worth; but if you are overleveraged and have too much debt, it can decrease your life-time giving potential. After all, every dollar you pay in interest and finance charges is one less dollar that can be used for giving. Plus, reducing debt can bring flexibility and open doors of opportunity that wouldn't be there otherwise.

This is where it's important to take the long view. I remember when I was dating my wife just after college, when we were moving toward marriage and starting to share our financial lives with each other. At the time, I was giving about 30% of my income to charity and trying to work that higher; meanwhile, I also had about $45K in student loan debt, which was a huge shock to her. She laid down an ultimatum to dial back the charitable giving to a typical 10% tithe and pay off the debt first, which I did, working multiple jobs to pay off the debt in just under two years. Looking back, this was wisdom on her part, because getting that debt paid off put me in a financial position that allowed me to go to business school and significantly increase my income, so that we are now able to give much more than I thought possible back then. She was shining a light on a blind spot I didn't even realize I had.

If you are deeply in debt and need to focus on paying some of it down first, Dave Ramsey's Baby Steps[10] are a pretty good framework for how to think about aggressively getting out from under that debt. I won't go into this system deeply, as the focus of this book picks up more after your debt is under control, but I will explain the basic concept. According to Dave's snowball method, you begin by listing out all your debts (except for your mortgage) in ascending order by balance size. After making minimum payments on all the other debts, you put any extra funds toward paying off

10   https://www.daveramsey.com/dave-ramsey-7-baby-steps

the smallest debt first. Then, once that debt is paid off, you take any money you were putting toward that debt and start applying it to the next smallest debt, then you continue with this until you are debt-free. This snowball effect leverages our own psychology to keep us motivated, as evidenced by a growing body of behavioral psychology research[11]. Additionally, a good financial advisor can provide a more customized roadmap for how much of your budget should go toward paying off debts and which debts to prioritize.

SAVING FOR RETIREMENT

In my years of experience working with clients of all different ages, I have observed that, on the front end of their careers, most people tend to overestimate how long they will work. Then, at some point, people start to just wear down, perhaps growing weary of the politics that inevitably infuses any organization comprised of human beings. Or they have ambitions to move on and spend the remainder of their lives doing other things, like volunteer work. Or they get outcompeted or forced out of the job market due to age-based biases or to make

---

11   https://academic.oup.com/jcr/article-abstract/43/3/
      460/2200459

way for a successor. Now, don't get me wrong, I've worked with plenty of people who absolutely love what they do for a living and work until they drop dead, but in my experience, those are the exceptions. In my experience, by the time most people reach retirement age, even if they don't want to retire, they at least recognize they will need to at some point.

If you have not been diligent in saving for this eventuality, you can end up in a position where you're having to work for much longer than you want to, even if just part-time. And due to health limitations or diminishing career opportunities, this can often mean earning less in these later years than you may have grown accustomed to in your peak earning years. All of this can translate into having to work just to meet your needs in these retirement years, which - needless to say - will constrain your lifetime giving impact.

If, on the other hand, you leverage the power of compound growth, the time value of money ensures that even modest sums saved regularly in your 20's and 30's will grow many multiples by retirement age, typically providing much more than needed to support your living needs in retirement and leaving plenty of wealth surplus for legacy goals, as shown on the next page.

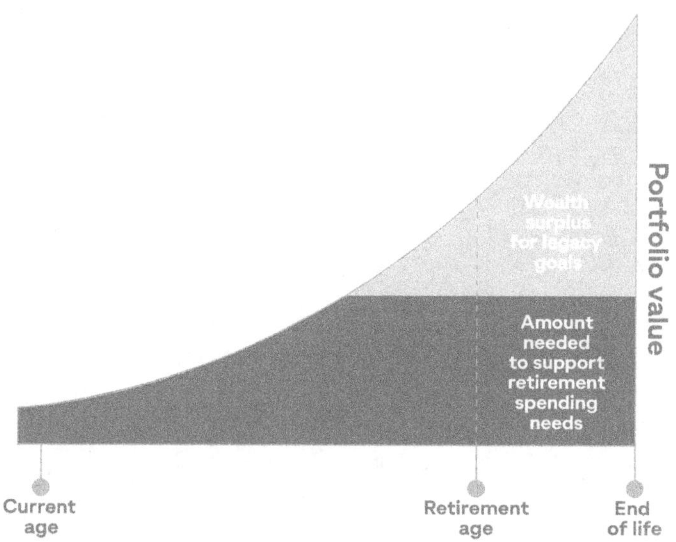

The general rule of thumb for ideal retirement savings is 15-20% of your income[12], but a good financial advisor can create a more personalized plan so you know exactly how much you need to be saving to meet your retirement spending and legacy goals. On this note, let's segue into legacy planning strategies in the accumulation years.

---

12 https://www.fidelity.com/viewpoints/retirement/how-much-money-should-I-save#:~:text=Fidelity's%20 rule%20of%20thumb%3A%20Aim,may%20get%20 from%20your%20employer.

PLANNING STRATEGY IN ACCUMULATION YEARS

~Ages 20-50

INTRO

Once the foundation is laid with an adequate cash emergency fund, the necessary insurance, responsible debt management, and a savings plan for retirement, then we can begin to think more strategically about legacy planning. This is where things start to get interesting, where we start to build on that foundation through analyzing existing laws and tax code to make informed decisions in service of this very specific goal of maximizing lifetime legacy giving.

I'll note here that a common theme in maximizing lifetime legacy giving is minimizing taxes and for good reason. Morningstar research[13] has shown that the average investor lost 1-2% of return annually to federal income taxes from 1926 to 2018. Two percent of extra return annually on a hypothetical portfolio of $100K could result in an additional $1 million after 40 years[14]. That is a lot of wealth surplus that could be used toward legacy goals!

Fortunately, lawmakers have generally recognized the value that charities and non-profits bring to society, so charitable giving is encouraged through favorable tax laws. Thus, for those of us interested in charitable legacy planning, one of the major objectives before us is to understand the tax code as it pertains to charitable giving and navigate it wisely. Effective tax planning is a long-term strategy, which is why it is important to be intentional about it as early in your career as possible.

Another common theme I will come back to in this book many times is using *leverage* to increase the giving impact of each dollar of wealth. Whether

---

13   https://advisor.mp.morningstar.com/resourceDownlo ad?type=publicForms&id=3f9dff3c-f085-47a1-98ba-0bc008df9f25

14   This is for illustrative purposes only to show the effect of 2% return compounded annually.

it is leveraging the power of low-cost debt, like mortgages, or leveraging the power of tax-free compound growth over time, the goal here is to increase the legacy giving Return on Investment (ROI) of our wealth.

QUALIFIED CHARITABLE DISTRIBUTIONS

One of the most powerful charitable giving incentives in the tax code is Qualified Charitable Distributions (QCDs) from pre-tax (i.e. Traditional and Rollover) Individual Retirement Accounts (IRAs). I provide more detail about why these are so powerful in the Retirement chapter, so feel free to reference that for additional context. For the time being, though, just know that in retirement, starting at age 70½, you can make up to $100K per year of charitable donations from your pre-tax retirement savings. Essentially, what this means is you are taking money that has never been taxed, growing it tax-deferred, then giving that compounded growth to charity, at which point you get another tax-deduction, thereby avoiding taxation on those distributions.

Traditional and Roth IRA contributions both receive a *double* tax benefit. For Traditional, you get a tax deduction at the point of contribution, as well as tax-deferred growth over time, but you must pay taxes at the point of distribution. For Roth, you don't get to deduct your contributions, but you get tax-deferred growth over time, and then you avoid having to pay taxes on the distributions. QCDs, on the other hand, give you a *triple* tax benefit because of the ability to avoid taxation on distributions from your Traditional IRA that would otherwise be taxable. We are now getting to a point of leveraging not just the power of compound growth or even *tax-deferred* compound growth, but of *tax-free* compound growth, to super-size your lifetime giving impact.

An important nuance here is that the QCD limit[15] is $100K *per individual* per year. This means that if you are married, you can give $100K per year of QCDs, and your spouse can give another $100K per year. The planning opportunity here, then, is to maximize both spouses' ability to make QCDs in retirement by finding ways to maximize pre-tax retirement contributions for both spouses, even if one spouse doesn't have earned income.

---

15   https://www.fidelitycharitable.org/guidance/philanthropy/qualified-charitable-distribution.html#:~:text=An%20individual%20donor%20can%20contribute,all%20IRAs%20in%20a%20year

MAXIMIZING PRE-TAX RETIREMENT CONTRIBUTIONS

Maximizing pre-tax retirement contributions is most commonly achieved through contributing to workplace 401k or 403b plans, if offered by your employer. For married couples where both spouses work, both spouses may contribute to their respective 401k or 403b plans. After leaving that employer or retiring, this money can be then rolled over to an IRA, making it available to be used for QCDs.

For relatively low earners, start by just contributing enough to get your full employer match (assuming there is one), otherwise you are leaving free money on the table. Again, the idea is to leverage the employer match to get a higher ROI on your investment dollars, which translates to increased wealth surplus available for legacy giving in retirement. As discretionary income increases, you can increase your retirement contributions beyond the employer match, up to the annual pre-tax contribution limit[16], which in 2021 is $19.5K, plus $6.5K catchup contribution for folks age 50 and over.

---

16   https://www.irs.gov/retirement-plans/401k-plans-deferrals-and-matching-when-compensation-exceeds-the-annual-limit#:~:text=Compensation%20and%20contribution%20limits%20are,g)%20and%20414(v)

For high earners with the ability to save even beyond these limits, you can still make non-deductible contributions, up to the combined employer and employee contribution limit of $58K, assuming your employer allows it. These non-deductible contributions are post-tax, but the earnings on them are pre-tax[17]. So, as the earnings compound over time, they can be used for QCDs in retirement, while the post-tax contributions can be rolled over to a Roth IRA (this is called a "mega back door Roth" strategy[18]) and used to live on in retirement or for inheritance goals. And again, if both spouses are maximizing their contributions, this could be a combined $116K in employer plan savings each and every year, plus catch-up contributions for folks 50 and over.

One caveat here: by saving with non-deductible contributions into an IRA as opposed to saving into a regular taxable account, the earnings will be taxed as ordinary income rather than capital gains, which are taxed at lower rates than ordinary income. Because of this, many tax accountants will advise you against doing non-deductible

---

17   https://www.fidelity.com/viewpoints/retirement/401k-contributions

18   https://www.thinkadvisor.com/2020/06/29/the-mega-backdoor-roth-explained/

IRA contributions. But, if you have strong charitable goals and will be using this money for QCDs, what rate the earnings are taxed at is not a concern because the distributions will be tax-free anyway.

In the case of a married couple where only one spouse earns income, the working spouse can still make what are called "spousal IRA contributions"[19] on behalf of their non-working spouse. So long as the couple files taxes jointly and total earned income is above the annual contribution limit for both spouses combined, both spouses can max out their IRA contributions for the year.

HEALTH SAVINGS ACCOUNTS

Since we've just talked about the triple tax benefits of QCDs, I would be remiss if I didn't mention Health Savings Accounts (HSAs). HSAs were created in 2003 and can only be used in conjunction with a high deductible health plan (HDHP), but they are becoming increasingly common[20]. If you

---

19   https://www.marketwatch.com/story/how-to-take-advantage-of-spousal-iras-2015-02-24

20   https://www.mayoclinic.org/healthy-lifestyle/consumer-health/in-depth/health-savings-accounts/art-20044058

have an HDHP, you can save money into an associated HSA, up to the annual limits[21], which are in the same ballpark as IRA contribution limits.

The beauty of an HSA is that it has a triple tax benefit, similar to a Traditional IRA and Roth IRA combined. In other words, you get to deduct your contributions to the HSA, the money in the HSA can be invested and grow tax-deferred over time, and withdrawals from the HSA are tax-free so long as they are used for qualified medical expenses. So, if you're in a position where you can pay any medical expenses out of pocket and leave your HSA contributions to grow over time, your HSA can be treated like a super-IRA, with medical expenses in retirement covered by money from the HSA, and other life expenses in retirement covered by other assets. Again, the goal here is to leverage the power of tax-free compound growth to increase the wealth that will be used for legacy giving down the road.

---

21   https://www.kiplinger.com/personal-finance/insurance/health-insurance/health-savings-accounts/601415/hsa-limits-and-minimums

EMPLOYER CHARITABLE MATCHING PROGRAMS

I have previously mentioned this idea of using leverage to increase the legacy giving Return on Investment (ROI) of our wealth. One powerful and often overlooked way to do this is by leveraging employer charitable matching programs, which many large employers have now begun to offer.

I remember when this light bulb first went off for me. I was focused on leveraging tax-free compound growth to increase the charitable giving ROI of my retirement savings dollars, which might increase the ROI to 15% annually, and that's being generous. Then it occurred to me that by leveraging the charitable matching program of my employer at the time, which matched 50% of all charitable giving by its employees, I would be getting an immediate 50% charitable giving ROI!

So, if you genuinely want to maximize your charitable giving impact, see if your employer offers a program like this, and if so, utilize it! The program offered by my employer at the time included every charitable organization imaginable, so I was able to move all my existing charitable giving onto the program's platform.

SELF-EMPLOYED INDIVIDUALS

For small business owners with no full-time employees other than the owner (and spouse, if the spouse is involved with the business), there are some unique opportunities for maximizing pre-tax retirement contributions, again with the goal of creating as much wealth surplus for legacy giving as possible. Foremost among them is the ability to utilize an individual 401k[22], or i401k, to maximize pre-tax retirement contributions for both the business owner and their spouse. SEP IRA's and SIMPLE IRA's are also an option for self-employed individuals, but i401ks generally offer greater annual contributions and bigger tax deductions[23], depending on your income.

QCDs can only be made from IRA accounts, but IRAs typically have much lower contribution limits than 401ks do. This is why I focused so much in the previous section on maximizing contributions to employer-sponsored 401k or 403b plans, and then rolling that money over to a Rollover IRA in retirement. For self-employed individuals, an i401k can serve the same purpose, as it has

---

22   https://investor.vanguard.com/small-business-retirement-plans/individual-solo-401k

23   https://www.forbes.com/advisor/retirement/sep-ira-vs-solo-401k/

the same contribution limits as an employer-sponsored 401k[24], and can then be rolled over to an IRA in retirement to take advantage of an IRA's QCD capabilities.

Depending on how your small business is structured, your spouse can also be included in the i401k[25] and make his or her own contributions, again opening up the ability to save up to $116K per married couple in pre-tax contributions annually, plus catch-up contributions for those 50 and over. When it comes to deciding on the right business structure to use for you and your spouse to both participate, always check with your CPA. The Small Business Administration has a good resource[26] to get you started.

---

24 https://investor.vanguard.com/small-business-retirement-plans/individual-solo-401k

25 https://www.solo401k.com/blog/how-to-include-your-spouse-in-your-solo-401k/

26 https://www.sba.gov/business-guide/launch-your-business/choose-business-structure

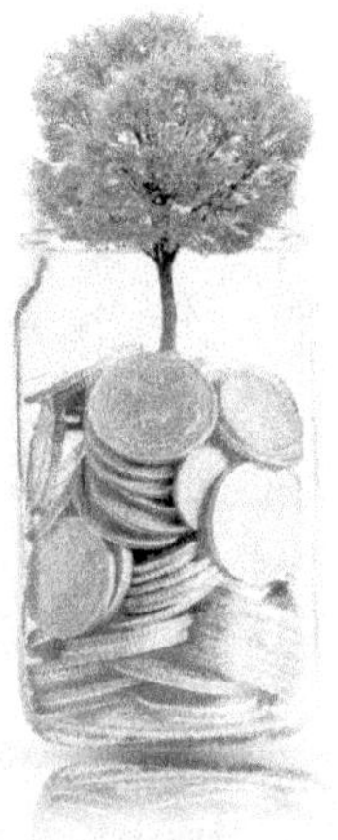

PLANNING STRATEGY IN PRE-RETIREMENT YEARS

~Ages 50-65

. . . .

INTRO

By this stage of life, most people have gotten debt under control and have begun to accumulate some assets, which means financial planning needs have started to evolve. If you have strong charitable giving goals, you are probably starting to give larger and larger amounts as your discretionary wealth increases, and this is where you can start to get really creative with your planned giving to maximize legacy impact. In this stage, in addition to continuing to leverage employer charitable matching programs (if offered) and tax-free compound growth on your retirement contributions while you still have earned income, there are other things to consider and opportunities that can be leveraged to increase your legacy giving ROI, which we will cover in this chapter.

INVESTMENT PHILOSOPHY AND PORTFOLIO CONSTRUCTION

How a portfolio is constructed and the investment philosophy that is followed has huge implications for the amount of wealth surplus leftover for legacy giving. The principles here could apply to investing at any life stage, but I am putting it in the pre-retiree chapter because this is when portfolios typically get larger, and the ramifications of portfolio management become greater the larger your portfolio grows.

Carl Richards has a great sketch that I think perfectly illustrates sound investment philosophy. It is a Venn diagram, with two overlapping circles. One of the circles is titled "Things that matter", while the other circle is titled "Things you can control". It is the middle overlap area – the things we can control that actually affect portfolio performance – that we want to focus on when it comes to investing.

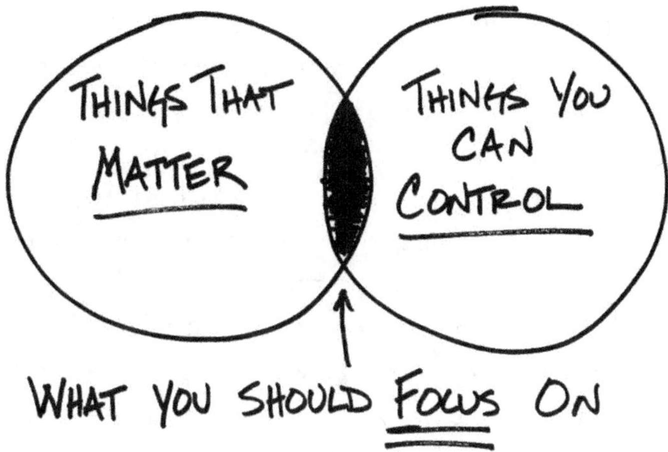

There are plenty of things that affect your investment performance that you have no control over, like what the Fed is doing with interest rates, the inflation rate, or how fast the economy is growing. Since you can't control them there's no use worrying about them. These factors define the field of play for all investors and set boundaries on the investment performance you can expect to see in your portfolio. For example, there is no escaping the gravitational pull of a low interest rate environment, so it is better to accept this reality and adapt rather than trying to fight it by "reaching for yield", which requires compromising diversification.

So, what is in the middle overlap area of that Venn diagram? Well, for starters, diversification and cost. These are two things we have direct control over that have huge implications for long-term investment performance, which means we really want to get them right. Whenever I construct portfolios for clients, one of my overarching goals is optimize the risk/return relationship of the portfolio. In other words, I want to get the most return for a given level of risk. Regardless of where we decide to land on the risk spectrum from conservative to aggressive, I want to make sure we're squeezing every last drop of return out of each increment of risk we're taking on. And the way we do that is primarily through maximizing diversification and minimizing costs (including minimizing taxes). This is most easily accomplished with broadly diversified, low-cost index funds, though there are exceptions.

Another factor in the middle of that Venn diagram is rebalancing regularly. I think of investing kind of like gardening. If you plant a garden and then walk away and forget about it, eventually that garden will become overrun with pests and weeds, making it less productive and fruitful than if you had actively tended to it. Similarly, with investing, if you want your portfolio to be as productive and fruitful as possible, there is basic portfolio hygiene required, and rebalancing is a big part of that.

Over time, as markets fluctuate, your stocks will grow faster than your bonds or cash, so your portfolio will tend to drift more aggressive and become stock heavy. Rebalancing involves periodically selling the relatively outperforming asset and buying the relatively underperforming asset to stay on track with the target allocation. Not only does this ensure you stay within the appropriate risk range, but every time you rebalance you are effectively selling high and buying low – not a bad formula for investment success.

Finally, another factor I would place in the middle area of that Venn diagram is maintaining discipline over the long term. The markets have always gone up over the long term and are exceedingly likely to continue rising in the future. It is a fundamental truth of market dynamics: in order to induce you to take on the risk of investing in the markets, the markets must compensate you in the form of some sort of positive return over time. If that were not the case - if you were expected to lose money in the markets over the long term - nobody would invest, and the markets would cease to function. The key to long term investment success is staying invested throughout the ups and downs to capture the long-term market return.

Having said that, we are all human beings subject to human emotions, so maintaining discipline in the face of market downturns is never easy.

Determining the appropriate portfolio allocation is more of an art than a science because we're trying to thread a needle. On the one hand, we want to have enough equity in your portfolio to achieve the growth needed to meet your future spending and legacy goals (stocks are the growth engine of a portfolio, after all). But, on the other hand, we also want to make sure your portfolio is not so aggressive that there is more volatility than you can handle in a down market. Too much volatility in your portfolio during a down market may tempt you to sell out of the market, which only short-circuits the process of capturing the long-term market return and typically does more harm than good.

Emotions and investing don't mix. The following graph visualizes research[27] showing that the average investor underperforms the stock market by 2-4% annually (that's a big bite out of your future legacy giving when compounded over many years!), and it's typically because emotions have clouded the investor's judgment. The investor who panics in a down market and pulls out of the market usually ends up locking in losses, and by the time they feel more comfortable getting back into the market, most of the recovery has already happened. So, they

---

27   https://www.thebalance.com/why-average-investors-earn-below-average-market-returns-2388519

end up shooting themselves in the foot on the way down and on the way back up. Fortunately, a good financial advisor can serve as an emotional circuit breaker; since they don't have the same emotional connection to your portfolio that you do, they can help you to maintain a long-term perspective.

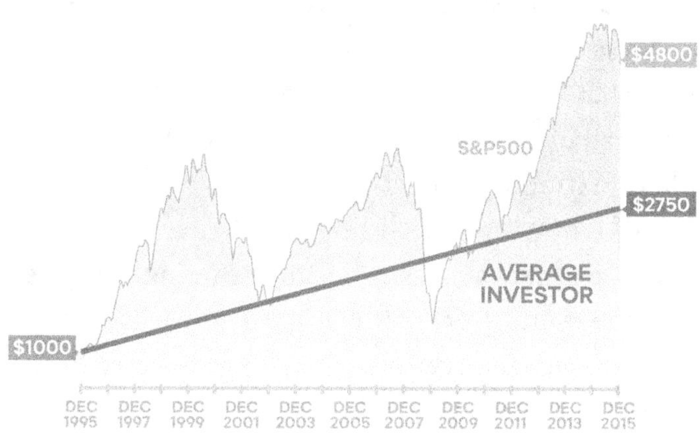

NON-RETIREMENT SAVINGS

If you have reached a point of maxing out retirement savings vehicles like 401ks and IRAs and you still have discretionary income to save, we want to be strategic about the next best places to save, keeping in mind your legacy goals.

The thoughts of some investors may immediately turn to tax-deferred annuities, which allow your annuity investments to grow tax-deferred, providing one half of the double tax advantage of an IRA. While this can a viable option for testamentary giving (giving done after your death), annuities aren't the best vehicle for charitable giving during your lifetime[28], because unlike Qualified Charitable Distributions from an IRA, all of the annuity's gains that received tax-deferral over the years have to be reported as income in the year the gift is made. Now, the deduction for the charitable donation would offset this income spike, but it still leaves you with little tax benefit. It could even be a net tax harm because the higher gross income could hurt your eligibility for other tax credits and deductions or drive your Medicare premiums higher.

At this point, aside from tax-advantaged savings vehicles for specific purposes (for example, contributing to a 529, which can only be used for qualified education expenses), your only remaining option is saving in a regular, taxable (non-tax advantaged) brokerage account. However, as we'll explore in the next couple of sections, there are still strategies that can be used here to leverage these accounts and maximize your legacy giving ROI.

---

28   https://finance.zacks.com/transfer-ownership-nonqualified-annuity-11540.html

ASSET LOCATION

One caveat I need to make upfront here: any time we deal with topics that touch upon taxes, none of the content in this book should be construed as tax advice. Please discuss these strategies with your tax advisor first. Having said that, when using taxable brokerage accounts, it is important to recognize that not all investments are as tax efficient as others. Given that taxable brokerage accounts lack the tax shelter inherent to an IRA, we need to be strategic about which assets we're placing in these accounts; this is called asset location[29].

For example, bonds tend to be tax-inefficient relative to stocks, so we want to avoid having bonds in taxable accounts, if possible. Most of the return of a bond is in the form of interest that gets kicked off over time. That interest is fully taxable at ordinary income rates, so it just gets added on top of all other income and taxed at your highest marginal rate. The pre-retirement years represent peak earning years for most people, so this interest can often be taxed at very high rates if not sheltered from taxes in an IRA.

On the other hand, most of the return for equities is in the form of growth over time, and those capital

---

29   https://www.investopedia.com/articles/tax/08/asset-location.asp

gains are not taxed until those stock positions are sold, so there is already some tax-deferral baked in. Even the dividends that get kicked off from equities are taxed at the lower capital gains rates if the dividends are considered qualified, and most dividends from US corporations are qualified[30].

Some may wonder about using tax-exempt municipal bonds in a taxable account to avoid paying taxes on the interest. Keep in mind, though, that municipal bonds have a discounted yield relative to taxable bonds. If a given taxable bond pays 3% interest, an equivalent municipal bond may only pay 2.5% because the municipalities issuing these bonds know you don't have to pay taxes on that interest, so the municipal market supports a lower yield. Tax-exempt municipal bonds only make sense when you're in a high enough tax bracket to justify that lower yield, and Morningstar research[31] indicates this threshold is crossed when you get into the 32% federal bracket. Even then, you're still better off using taxable bonds in a tax-sheltered IRA if you have the available IRA shelf space.

---

30 https://www.investopedia.com/terms/q/qualifieddividend.asp

31 https://www.morningstar.com/articles/961786/should-you-own-a-muni-fund

Something else to keep in mind when it comes to asset location is the difference between passively managed funds and actively managed funds. With active funds, the fund manager is continually buying and selling securities to try to outperform a given index. Any gains realized from the fund manager's trading activity get passed along to you in the form of capital gains distributions, which are taxable to you. On the other hand, a passive fund seeks to closely track an index to capture the market return, so, assuming the index is relatively stable, there is very little internal trading activity, or turnover. This makes active funds inherently less tax efficient than passive funds, meaning you generally want to avoid using active funds in a taxable account.

TAX LOSS HARVESTING

As you make contributions to a regular, taxable brokerage account, you will buy a given security (let's assume stock/equity mutual funds for the moment) on different dates over time. This means you'll have several lots, which are just the same security purchased on different dates, typically with different purchase prices due to market fluctuation. In taxable brokerage accounts, lot-level trading features prominently in strategies for lowering taxes and maximizing charitable giving impact.

You must change your cost basis election with your brokerage firm to take advantage of this, but I would argue it's worth it. Most brokerage firms default your cost basis election to "Average Cost", meaning every time you sell a security, it uses the average cost basis across all the lots of that security to determine the taxable gains being realized. If you change the cost basis election to "Specific Identification", you are then able to specifically identify which lots to sell to produce the desired tax consequence.

For example, let's assume you purchase ABC stock fund for $100/share today. Next year, it goes up to $130/share, and you purchase another lot at that price. Then, over time, it falls back down to $110/share. The first lot, with the cost basis of only $100, still has unrealized gains of $10/share, while the second lot has unrealized *losses* of $20/share. As painful as it can be to see losses in your portfolio, the silver lining is that it presents opportunities for tax loss harvesting.

In the scenario above, with "Specific Identification" elected, we can sell the second lot and lock in that $20/share loss to reduce your taxable income. Now, in tax loss harvesting scenarios like this, you generally don't want to just leave the sale proceeds in cash, because then you miss out on the inevitable market recovery. However, you can't purchase back into ABC stock fund within 30 days, or the IRS considers it a wash sale[32], and the loss is disallowed.

The workaround is to use the proceeds to purchase into a surrogate fund – let's call it XYZ stock fund - that is substantially similar, but different enough to get around the wash sale rules. This allows you to lock in the losses from a tax perspective, but not from an investment perspective – it's like having your cake and eating it, too. Then, after that 30-day wash sale window has closed, you can always choose to unwind this trade and move back into the original ABC stock fund.

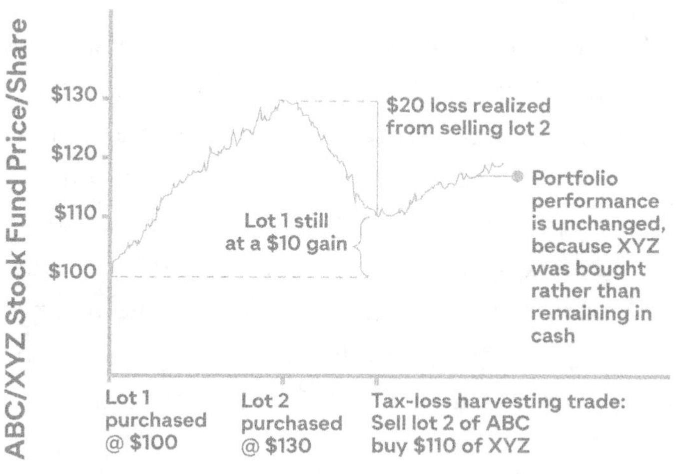

---

32 https://www.fidelity.com/learning-center/personal-finance/wash-sales-rules-tax

Capital losses harvested in this way can be used as a deduction against ordinary income (e.g. employment income) - which is taxed at higher rates than capital gains - only up to $3K/year, while the rest can be used to offset capital gain income. Any losses leftover after offsetting ordinary and capital gain income can then be carried forward into future tax years indefinitely[33]. These harvested losses help to minimize taxes, again helping to create more wealth surplus that can be used for legacy giving.

GIFTING APPRECIATED SECURITIES

When it comes time to make charitable gifts, many people just gift cash. However, if you're starting to build up significant assets in a taxable brokerage account and your investments are presumably growing over time, just gifting cash misses out on a valuable opportunity. By gifting these appreciated securities from your taxable brokerage account instead, you get a double tax benefit: you get the charitable deduction on the full amount gifted to

---

33 https://www.investopedia.com/terms/c/capital-loss-carryover.asp#:~:text=Net%20capital%20losses%20in%20excess,for%20the%20beneficial%20tax%20treatment.

charity and avoid ever having to pay taxes on the gains. The charity can then sell the securities tax-free to convert the gift to cash. And if you want, you can always use your cash to buy additional shares of the same securities you just gifted, effectively stepping up your cost basis to the current market value.

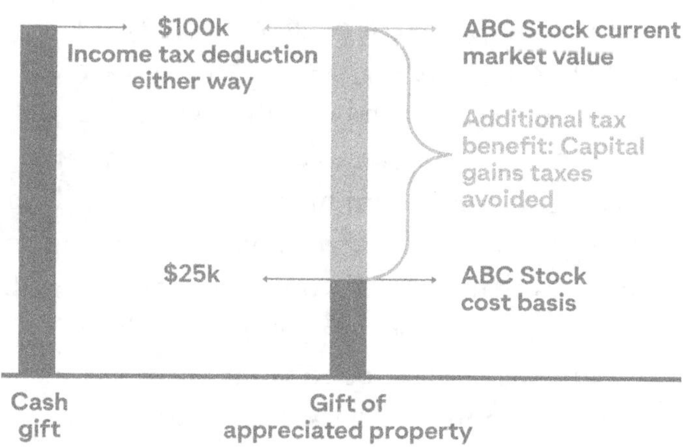

And again, the "Specific Identification" cost basis election allows us to precisely choose the most highly appreciated lots to use for charitable gifting, thereby minimizing tax liability and maximizing charitable giving potential. Conversely, positions with unrealized losses should be sold first, before given to charity, so you reap the tax benefit of the realized loss. This type of precision gifting can be used strategically, like a surgeon's scalpel, to bring taxable income down into a desired tax bracket or below a target threshold to maintain eligibility for certain tax credits and deductions. It is, therefore, typically done near the end of the year when there is more clarity on total taxable income for the year.

One caveat here is that the tax deduction limit[34] for gifts of appreciated property is only 30% of adjusted gross income (AGI), while for cash gifts it is 60% of AGI (with both allowing a five-year carryforward for any unused deduction), meaning you can gift a higher amount in cash and still get the full tax benefit. However, if you're planning on gifting less than 30% of your gross income each year anyway, appreciated assets may be the way to go. Another planning opportunity is to gift large amounts of appreciated assets in years when you have taxable income spikes.

---

34   https://www.schwab.com/resource-center/insights/content/charitable-donations-the-basics-of-giving#:~:text=In%20generally%20your%20donation%20deduction,is%2030%25%20of%20your%20AGI.

DONOR ADVISED FUNDS AND CHARITABLE BUNCHING

Most charities have brokerage accounts into which they can receive gifts of appreciated securities, but another option is to use a Donor Advised Fund[35] (DAF). Compared to private foundations[36], DAFs are more accessible, have lower administrative expenses, and have higher tax deduction limits as a percentage of AGI. With a DAF, you just gift the appreciated securities to the DAF, sell the securities within the DAF, then give cash to the charities of your choice.

The other nice thing about a DAF is the flexibility it provides. The tax deduction occurs at the point of contributing to the DAF, but then the money can stay in the DAF until you're ready to make charitable gifts, for instance, after you've completed doing research on the charities to which you want to give. If you haven't decided on the charities you want to fund, Charity Navigator[37] may be a good place to start. Additionally, the IRS has an online search tool called Tax Exempt Organization

---

35   https://www.vanguardcharitable.org/giving-with-vc/how-it-works

36   https://www.nptrust.org/donor-advised-funds/daf-vs-foundation/

37   https://www.charitynavigator.org/

Search[38] that makes it easy to see if an organization to which you're considering contributing qualifies for tax-deductible donations.

The flexibility of the DAF also facilitates a unique planning opportunity called charitable bunching[39]. The 2017 tax reform bill, called the Tax Cuts and Jobs Act, significantly increased the standard deduction, dropping the number of tax returns[40] with itemized deductions from ~31% before the tax reform to 13.7% in 2019. While great for the majority of filers who don't itemize, this has effectively diluted the potency of charitable deductions for those folks who regularly make charitable gifts. However, charitable bunching is one way to restore the power of charitable deductions.

Charitable bunching is when you make several years' worth of charitable gifts in one year, to get the full itemized deductions, and then just take the standard deduction in the other years. A DAF simplifies this charitable bunching, because you can make your multi-year gifts into the DAF (and get the full upfront tax deduction for the entire

---

38   https://apps.irs.gov/app/eos/

39   https://www.donorstrust.org/donor-advised-funds/bunching-strategy-charitable-giving/

40   https://taxfoundation.org/standard-deduction-itemized-deductions-current-law-2019/

multi-year gift), and then distribute the cash to charity over the ensuing years.

There is one interesting corollary to this charitable bunching strategy. The CARES act and follow-on Covid pandemic stimulus legislation created a unique, limited-time opportunity to deduct 100% of AGI for cash charitable donations in 2020 and 2021, with the limit currently set to revert to the previous limit of 60% of AGI starting in 2022. This means if you're thinking about implementing a charitable bunching strategy, 2020 and 2021 are great years to do your giving. Having said that, it may not be advisable to use charitable deductions against all your gross income in one year[41], because then you're offsetting income that will be taxed at much lower rates anyway.

---

41 https://www.kitces.com/blog/100-agi-charitable-deduction-limit-cash-qualified-contribution/

PLANNING STRATEGY IN RETIREMENT YEARS

~Ages 65+

. . . .

INTRO

When it comes to legacy giving, the retirement years are where most of the action is because it's typically when people reach their financial asset peak and have the most to give. For the legacy builder, this is where all your decades of planning come into full bloom, where you reap the harvest from your years of quietly and faithfully sowing the seeds of a financial legacy.

QUALIFIED CHARITABLE DISTRIBUTIONS

I began to talk about Qualified Charitable Distributions (QCDs) in the Accumulation chapter to get younger accumulators to start thinking about a long-term strategy, centered around QCDs, to maximize charitable giving. Feel free to reference that section for additional information but given that QCDs aren't even an option until you turn 70½, I wanted to devote space in this chapter to some of the mechanics of QCDs and why they are so powerful.

Let's begin with answering the question - what makes a QCD *qualified* in the first place? Well, there are a few requirements[42] for a distribution from your IRA to be considered a *Qualified* Charitable Distribution:

1. You must be at least 70½.

2. Qualifying charitable gifts can only be made to certain types of eligible public charities, meaning gifts to your donor-advised fund, private foundation, or split-interest charitable trusts

---

42 https://www.kitces.com/blog/qualified-charitable-distribution-qcd-from-ira-to-satisfy-rmd-rules-and-requirements/

(Charitable Lead Trusts and Charitable Remainder Trusts) are ineligible.

3. Donation checks must be made payable from the IRA directly to the charitable entity rather than to the IRA owner, although the check can be sent to the IRA owner and then forwarded to the charity.

4. QCDs can total a maximum of $100K per individual, per year.

The starting point for any discussion on why QCDs are so powerful is that they count toward your Required Minimum Distributions (RMDs). Uncle Sam, in his benevolence, allows tax-deferred savings into IRAs and 401ks as an incentive to get people to save for retirement. But he does not allow this tax deferral to go on indefinitely; at some point, he wants his cut. This is where RMDs come in. Starting at age 72 (the recently enacted SECURE act[43] raised the RMD age from 70½ to 72), the IRS requires you to distribute a percentage of the balance on your pre-tax retirement accounts every year, and that percentage increases every year for the remainder of your life. These

---

43 https://www.irs.gov/retirement-plans/retirement-plans-faqs-regarding-required-minimum-distributions#:~:text=The%20Secure%20Act%20made%20major,year%20after%20you%20reach%2072.

distributions are fully taxable as ordinary income (i.e. added on top of all other income and taxed at your highest marginal rates), so this can start to put a tax squeeze on retirees if they haven't planned strategically for this eventuality.

To make matters worse, the SECURE act also changed the RMD rules for heirs[44] who eventually inherit these IRAs. Whereas heirs used to be able to stretch out their own RMDs on inherited IRAs over their lifetime, they now must fully distribute all assets from the inherited IRA within 10 years of the original IRA owner's death. On average, an heir receiving inherited IRA assets is in their late 40's/early 50's[45] and typically in their peak earning years. So, now over a 10-year period when they are likely in the highest earning years of their career, they must take much larger RMDs that get added on top of their income and taxed at their highest marginal rates. When it comes to planning for inheritance goals, this is not an ideal situation

---

44 https://www.wealthmanagement.com/estate-planning/secure-act-sets-inherited-ira-rmd-complexity-advisors

45 https://www.businessinsider.com/personal-finance/older-americans-get-more-inheritances-use-for-retirement-2019-11#:~:text=The%20typical%20American%20heir%20is,puts%20the%20money%20toward%20retirement&text=Over%20the%20last%2030%20years,United%20Income%20from%20Capital%20One.

in which to put your heirs (although some retirees prefer to leave the tax burden with their heirs for various reasons).

Fortunately, QCDs offer significant relief for the charitably inclined, allowing you to divert large swaths of your pre-tax IRA money to charitable giving each year, leaving post-tax money to meet any inheritance goals. Of these post-tax accounts, Roth assets tend to be good for leaving to heirs because heirs receive the money tax-free. They will still have RMDs (again because Uncle Sam doesn't want those assets staying in the Roth account growing tax-free forever), but those distributions will be tax-free.

Appreciated securities in taxable brokerage accounts can also be good for bequeathing to heirs, because the cost basis on your holdings will be stepped up to the market value on the date of your death[46]. This step-up in basis exists in the tax code because finding out what someone's parents or grandparents paid for an asset can be an administrative nightmare. The net result of this rule is that any unrealized gains get wiped away for your heirs, leaving them with a clean slate (this is true as of this writing, but there is growing discussion

------

46 https://taxfoundation.org/step-up-in-basis/

among federal lawmakers about getting rid of this step-up in basis, although any change would likely be met with howls of resistance from CPAs and tax accountants, who would bear the brunt of having to help track down cost basis from many decades prior in some cases).

For illustration, let's say you purchased a share of stock for $100 many years ago, and it is worth $300 on the day you die. There is $200 of unrealized gains that would have been taxable if you sold that holding, but when it passes to your heirs, the cost basis gets stepped up from $100 to $300. They can now sell that stock without realizing any gains and having to pay taxes on it.

Before we leave the topic of RMDs, I should note (because I have found that many retirees haven't made this connection) that come RMD age, the IRS only requires you to distribute from the IRA so they can receive the tax revenue. The IRS does not require you to spend that money, so if you don't need it for your living needs, you can always reinvest it in a regular post-tax brokerage account and continue to grow your wealth surplus for legacy giving.

So, to summarize, QCDs effectively give your pre-tax IRAs a triple tax advantage by allowing you to deduct your contributions, grow the assets tax-deferred, and then distribute the QCDs free from the taxes that would otherwise be assessed through RMDs. And QCDs are an "above the line" deduction[47] rather than an itemized deduction, meaning you can benefit from the standard deduction and still get the full tax benefit of your charitable gifts. For example, as illustrated on the following page, let's say your gross income in a given tax year was $100K, and you gave $20K to charity. Let's also assume you file taxes jointly with your spouse and there are no further deductions to be itemized. If you just gave that $20K from non-IRA money, your gross income would be $100K. You would take the standard deduction of ~$24K (because it is higher than the $20K in itemized deductions for charitable giving), and your taxable income would be ~$76K. If, on the other hand, you make the $20K in charitable giving as QCDs, it would reduce your gross income from $100K down to $80K, you would again take the standard deduction of ~$24K, and your taxable income would now only be ~$56K.

Furthermore, because QCDs don't increase your adjusted gross income (AGI), they avoid pushing

---

47 https://blog.taxact.com/itemized-vs-above-line-deductions/

you into higher tax brackets that could potentially expose you to the Medicare surtax or increase the proportion of your Social Security income that is taxable. This also avoids potentially driving your Medicare premiums higher and reducing eligibility for certain tax credits and deductions that are tied to AGI.

	Normal charitable gift	Qualified charitable distribution
	$20k Gift to charity	
Gross income	$100k	$100k
"Above the line" deductions		-$20k
Adjusted gross income	$100k	$80k
"Below the line" deduction { Greater of itemized deductions or standard deduction	-$24k	-$24k
Taxable income	$76k	$56k

BASIC ESTATE PLANNING

A basic estate planning package typically includes a will, powers of attorney, advanced medical directives, guardianship instructions for surviving minors, etc. The need for at least basic estate planning is applicable to any life stage, but I am including it here, because the need becomes more acute the older you get and the larger your net worth grows. A quick caveat here before we begin, much of the content to follow touches on legal themes but should not be construed as legal advice; I intentionally speak about these topics in a generalized way, so please consult a qualified estate planning attorney familiar with the laws in your state for more specific guidance and for assistance in finalizing estate planning legal documents.

To better understand why estate planning is so critical to legacy building, let's begin by looking at what happens when you die intestate (without a will)[48]. When this happens, your assets become frozen until a probate judge is able to comb through every detail of your estate and apply the intestacy laws of the state where you reside. This process can be time-consuming, expensive and emotionally draining for your heirs, not to mention that it is highly unlikely any of your assets would end up supporting charitable goals in the absence of legally binding documents clearly expressing your desire that they do so.

A will gives you the chance to direct probate proceedings according to your wishes, and it tends to make for a smoother process, although it can still be time-consuming and expensive, depending on the

---

48   https://trustandwill.com/learn/dying-without-a-will

probate laws in your state and the size of your estate. In general, the larger the assets going through probate, the higher the legal fees involved[49], and most states now have simplified "shortcut" processes for small estates. The probate hearings[50] give all interested parties a chance to contest the will, or to the appointment of the executor, for instance. While important to preserve beneficiary rights, this can open the door for things to go sideways and start to go in directions you never would have intended. Additionally, the probate proceedings must be made public to notify creditors who have claims against the estate for money owed, potentially attracting unwanted public scrutiny; it is not uncommon for unscrupulous scammers[51] to monitor these public notices and prey upon vulnerable heirs.

Because of these drawbacks to probate, one of the major goals of estate planning is to bypass probate as much as possible, and there are several ways to do so. The simplest and, some would say, most

---

49   https://www.nolo.com/legal-encyclopedia/avoid-probate-how-to-30235.html

50   https://www.thebalance.com/what-is-probate-3505244#:~:text=Probate%20is%20the%20court%2D-supervised,estate%20to%20their%20rightful%20beneficiaries.

51   https://mmzlawyer.com/inheritance-and-probate-scams-to-watch-out-for/

extreme option (although not so extreme in the context of maximizing legacy impact) is to just give your assets away before you die. This calls to mind the adage, "do your giving while you're living, so you're knowing where it's going." We will discuss various vehicles for doing this giving in later sections of this chapter. I should say, significant inter vivos giving (giving while you're still alive) can be a great option for charitable giving, but it may not be the best option for inheritance goals, because your heirs don't get a step-up in basis[52]; your cost basis on the purchase of the asset would transfer to your heirs.

Another good way to bypass probate, which is probably familiar to most, is designating beneficiaries on IRAs, 401ks, life insurance policies, and annuities. You can even designate Payable on Death (POD) beneficiaries on bank accounts and Transfer on Death (TOD) beneficiaries on many taxable brokerage accounts, and some states allow you to designate beneficiaries on real estate deeds and motor vehicle titles. When you pass away, these assets pass directly to your beneficiaries without having to go through probate. To achieve both charitable legacy goals and inheritance legacy goals, QCDs from your IRAs can be a good complement to beneficiary

---

52 https://www.taxpolicycenter.org/briefing-book/what-difference-between-carryover-basis-and-step-basis

designations, whereby you do QCDs during your lifetime and designate heirs as beneficiaries of the remaining amounts at your death.

You can also add a joint owner[53] to a bank account, taxable brokerage account or a real estate deed, and provided that joint ownership includes rights of survivorship, when you pass away, ownership of the asset reverts fully to the surviving joint owner without having to go through probate. There are a couple of major drawbacks here, though. One is that you lose control over the assets when they pass to the joint owner, and the surviving joint owner is free to change the ultimate beneficiaries of the assets in a way you would never have intended. This highlights the importance of good communication with any joint owners to ensure you are on the same page regarding estate planning goals. The other major drawback is that if the joint owner passes away, gets divorced, or gets sued, the assets in your joint account with them could be part of their settlement.

A final option is to create a revocable living trust, which were invented as a way to bypass probate[54]. Once the trust is created, you then must take the

---

53   https://www.thebalance.com/ways-to-avoid-probate-3505251

54   https://www.nolo.com/legal-encyclopedia/avoid-probate-how-to-30235.html

next step of retitling assets to the trust, but once in the trust, those assets will pass according to the instructions in the trust document without having to go through probate. You retain the right to "revoke" that funding and move money in and out of the trust as needed; so, when you have a brokerage account tied to that trust, it functions exactly like a regular, taxable brokerage account, the only difference being that upon your death the assets will pass according to the trust document rather than your will via probate. Your brokerage company will help with retitling brokerage account assets to the trust, your estate planning attorney can help with retitling real estate deeds to the trust, and you can then retitle any other asset valuable enough to warrant the effort, including expensive jewelry, art collections, etc.

Additionally, a trust allows you to not only control who receives your assets, but the *timing* of the disposition of those assets. With a will, once your estate is settled in the probate process, any assets that pass through the will are immediately accessible to beneficiaries (heirs or charities), which can be problematic if they are not mature enough to steward that amount of wealth. There are countless stories throughout history of large windfalls proving ruinous to immature wealth stewards. In contrast, there is great flexibility in the distribution parameters you can set for a trust and, in many ways, you are limited only by your imagination.

GIFT & ESTATE TAXES

Another major goal of estate planning is minimizing exposure to transfer taxes (e.g. gift taxes assessed on transfers made during your lifetime and estate taxes assessed on post-death transfers). Again, every dollar of wealth surplus not paid to the IRS is one more dollar that can be used for legacy giving. Currently, federal transfer taxes top out at 40% of your estate above a certain combined lifetime gift/estate tax exemption threshold (known as the unified credit), and the 2017 tax reform raised this exemption amount[55] to $11.7 million per person and $23.4 million per married couple.

Obviously, very few estates will be subject to transfer taxes at these lofty exemption amounts, so it can be tempting to think this is not applicable. However, this unified credit is constantly changing based on the party in power in Washington, and raising the unified credit was one of the more controversial elements of the 2017 tax reform among Democrats.

---

55 https://www.irs.gov/businesses/small-businesses-self-employed/estate-tax

With Democrats taking control of the presidency, Senate and House in the 2020 elections, this unified credit threshold is likely to be reduced significantly, and the transfer tax rates are likely to go up, exposing a much broader swath of households to these taxes. Additionally, many states assess their own estate tax[56], often with much lower exemption thresholds, so this aspect of estate planning is still very much relevant. To err on the side of caution, it is generally best to assume the exemption amount is $1M, for instance, and plan accordingly to reduce the taxable estate.

Fortunately for those focused on giving much of their wealth to charitable causes, while charitable income tax deductions are limited to a percentage of your gross income, charitable estate tax deductions are unlimited[57]. In a sense, this makes transfer taxes optional for the committed charitable legacy builder.

Another important planning opportunity for inheritance legacy goals is making use of the annual

---

56 https://smartasset.com/taxes/all-about-the-estate-tax

57 https://sharpenet.com/blog/estate-tax-charitable-deduction/#:~:text=The%20income%20tax%20charitable%20deduction%20is,for%20gifts%20to%20U.S.%20charities.&text=Second%2C%20the%20estate%20tax%20charitable,course%2C%20subject%20to%20various%20limitations.

gift tax exclusion[58]. When you give a gift to someone for which you don't expect to receive fair payment, even if you sell something to someone below market value or loan money below market interest rates, that discounted amount qualifies as a gift under federal tax law. With the annual gift tax exclusion, you can give up to $15K per person, per year completely free of any gift tax implications (gifts to spouses are generally unlimited). This is per person, mind you, so you can give $15K each to children, sons-in-law or daughters-in-law, grandchildren, your neighbor down the street…anyone you want. If you are married, you and your spouse can combine your exclusion amounts to give a total of $30K per year. So, you can see how you can really start to whittle down your taxable estate if you are strategic about it. Any gift above this annual exclusion amount counts against your lifetime unified credit, beyond which your assets are exposed to gift and estate taxes.

We have talked extensively in previous chapters about minimizing exposure to income taxes, and I have now introduced the idea of minimizing exposure to transfer taxes. It is important to draw out this distinction, because whether your biggest tax reduction priority is minimizing income taxes

---

58   https://www.policygenius.com/taxes/guide-to-gift-tax/

or minimizing transfer taxes factors heavily into the decision of which legacy giving vehicle is most suitable, as we'll discuss in the following sections.

We have previously covered employer charitable matching programs, gifting appreciated property, charitable bunching with Donor Advised Funds, Qualified Charitable Distributions, etc., but there are some planned giving vehicles that might make sense for higher net worth legacy builders. As we turn our attention to these vehicles, we will start with some irrevocable trust arrangements (meaning assets placed into the trust are final and cannot be reversed) that could make sense at high enough wealth levels. I say "high enough wealth levels" because the downside with any irrevocable trust is the attorney fees to create the trust and the trustee fees for ongoing administration of the trust, so the trust funding levels must be high enough to justify these costs.

CHARITABLE LEAD TRUSTS

For high net worth folks with strong inheritance goals and strong charitable goals, a Charitable Lead Trust[59] (CLT) can be an attractive tool for

---

59 https://www.pgdc.com/pgdc/charitable-lead-trust

transferring assets to heirs with little or no transfer tax. Its distinctive advantage is that, in addition to serving as a vehicle through which to make large charitable distributions each year, it allows you to direct the ultimate disposition of the remaining trust assets at the end of the trust term, all while helping you achieve specific tax minimization objectives.

CLTs are a type of split-interest irrevocable trust where you, as the grantor, fund the trust (either during your lifetime or by your will) with assets that will pay ongoing income out to a charitable beneficiary for a set term. The assets remaining at the end of the trust term revert to you or another noncharitable beneficiary (i.e. heir). The trust term can be your lifetime or a fixed period (for example, 20 years), and charitable income payments can either be a fixed *sum* or a fixed *percentage* of trust assets each year. It's called a CLT because the charity has the lead interest, while noncharitable beneficiaries have the remainder interest. Because the charitable beneficiaries enjoy the certainty of a fixed stream of funding, CLTs can be a good vehicle for long-term charitable commitments and endowment funding.

There are two main types of CLTs: grantor CLTs, where the remaining assets at the end of the trust term revert to the grantor, and non-grantor CLTs, where the remaining assets pass to heirs. Grantor CLTs[60] can help address the challenge of too much taxable income in a specific calendar year, because they allow donors to consolidate charitable deductions for future donations into a larger deduction for a single year. Grantor CLTs provide grantors an upfront charitable income tax deduction for the present value of the annual charitable payments (although income generated from the trust assets each year is taxable to the grantor), but they have minimal impact on transfer taxes (because the remaining assets come back into the grantor's estate at the end of the trust term, so there is little shrinkage of the taxable estate).

Accordingly, grantor CLTs are often funded in years when the grantor has a big spike in taxable income, such as large windfalls from the sale of a business, or other one-time boosts to earnings. In low interest rate environments, the upfront charitable income tax deduction received from a grantor CLT can be 60-70% or more of the initial funding amount. With good investment management over the term of the trust, the donor can be expected to receive much of that original funding back.

---

60 https://www.pgcalc.com/support/knowledge-base/pg-calc-featured-articles/grantor-charitable-lead-trusts-why-they-sometimes

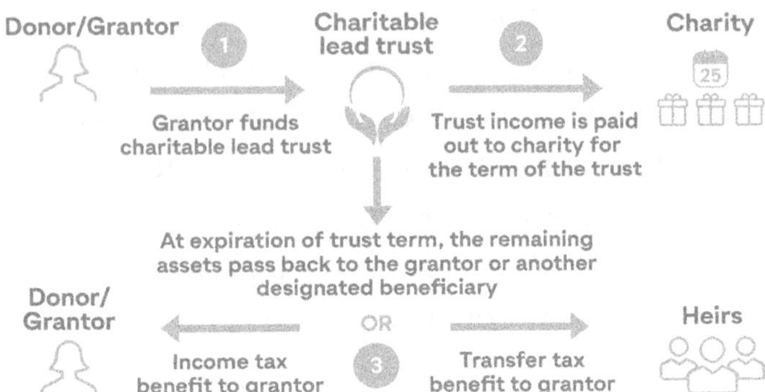

A non-grantor CLT is the most common type of CLT and helps to address the challenge of too much wealth at death, leading to exposure to transfer taxes, by giving the donor a transfer tax deduction for the present value of the stream of income that will be paid to charity during the trust term. By strategically structuring the term and the charitable payout, it's possible to receive a transfer tax deduction that perfectly offsets the trust funding amount. These assets pass on to heirs at the end of the trust term, so this is a good way to meet charitable goals while also shrinking taxable estates through transfer tax-free asset transfers to heirs. No income tax reduction benefit is provided, but in contrast to the grantor CLT, the annual income produced by the trust assets is not taxable to the grantor.

Depending on the type of CLT, it can be challenging or impossible to change charitable beneficiaries after the trust is established, and at the very least may require an amendment to the trust. In order to preserve greater flexibility here[61], a Donor Advised Fund can be a good complement to a CLT. By designating the DAF as the sole charitable beneficiary of the CLT, you can then advise the DAF to make grants to the charities of your choosing and change those charities at any time.

CHARITABLE REMAINDER TRUSTS

In some ways, a Charitable Remainder Trust[62] (CRT) is the inverse of a CLT. That's because non-charitable beneficiaries (i.e. you as the donor or your heirs) of a CRT retain the lead income interest, with the remaining assets at the end of the trust term passing to charity. Again, the trust is named after the charity's interest, in this case, the remainder interest. It can be an attractive option for otherwise motivated charitable legacy builders who

---

61   https://www.fidelitycharitable.org/guidance/philanthropy/charitable-lead-trusts.html

62   https://www.pgdc.com/pgdc/charitable-remainder-trusts

have concerns about inadvertently giving away too much of their assets to charity and exposing themselves to longevity risk (i.e. the risk of outliving their assets' ability to support them), because they can receive the income from the assets for the remainder of their lives before passing it along to their charitable beneficiaries. Additionally, charities benefit even before receiving the gift, because they have time to plan around the gift and lay the foundation for projects and initiatives that may be funded by it.

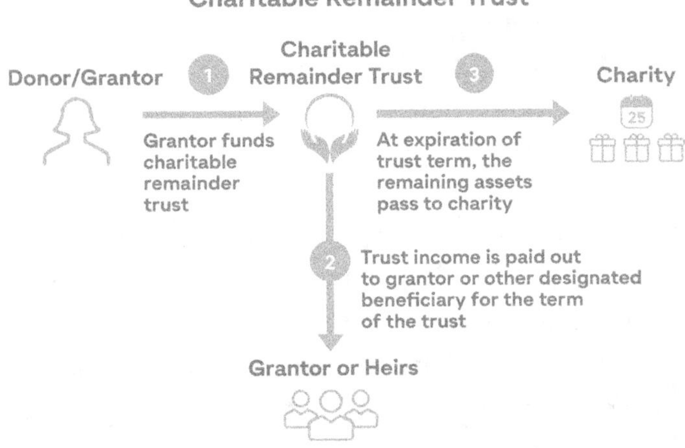

Unlike a CLT, a CRT is tax-exempt, so it is ideally funded with appreciated assets that can then be sold inside the trust. This saves the grantor the capital gains taxes from selling that appreciated property on his or her own, as well as providing an immediate charitable income tax deduction equal to the present value of the expected remaining assets that will pass to charity. The effect of these tax savings[63] means the grantor is likely to receive more annual income from assets placed into the trust than if he or she had not funded the trust, especially in low interest rate environments. Additionally, funding an irrevocable trust like a CRT shrinks the grantor's taxable estate, thereby minimizing exposure to transfer taxes. It also shrinks the probate estate (i.e. the portion of the estate passing through probate), so fewer assets can be contested by heirs or claimed by creditors.

CRTs can either be categorized as a Charitable Remainder Annuity Trust (CRAT), which pays out a fixed *sum* annually to the income beneficiaries, or a Charitable Remainder Unitrust (CRUT), which pays out a fixed *percentage* of the trust assets annually (meaning the payments can fluctuate depending on investment performance of the trust assets). A CRUT is generally more flexible[64], as it allows you to make additional funding

---

63 https://www.estateplanning.com/Understanding-Charitable-Remainder-Trusts/

64 https://actecfoundation.org/podcasts/charitable-remainder-trusts-faqs-crt/

contributions to the trust over time, if you so desire. A CRUT also allows for a variety of creative planning opportunities to delay income - for instance, until retirement when a grantor's taxable income is lower, or until such a time as the grantor moves from a high-income tax state to a lower-income tax state.

Like most trusts, a CRT can either be a living trust (created during the grantor's lifetime) or a testamentary trust (embedded in the will and only created at the grantor's death). When used as a testamentary trust, a CRT can receive your estate's remaining IRA assets so heirs can receive some income from it before going straight to charity, if you desire. Additionally, these distributions to your heirs can be stretched out over a longer time period than the 10 years within which your heirs are required to fully distribute inherited IRA assets[65]. The drawback to this strategy, of course, is that a testamentary trust is imbedded in the will until your death, so any assets going into the testamentary trust would still have to go through probate.

One caveat with any split-interest charitable trust like CLTs or CRTs is that, since the charitable interest of the trust is considered a gift "for the use

---

65   https://investor.vanguard.com/inherit/ira-rmd

of" charity rather than a gift "to" charity, the charitable income tax deduction is limited to just 30% of AGI for cash and 20% for appreciated assets. The good news is that there is a five-year carryforward for any unused charitable deduction. While they are not perfect solutions, CRTs can be a useful way to more thoughtfully time income taxation and leverage tax savings to subsidize your charitable giving.

IRREVOCABLE LIFE INSURANCE TRUSTS

For legacy builders who may have reservations about these strategies due to a fear of giving too much of their net worth to charity and leaving their heirs vulnerable, an Irrevocable Life Insurance Trust[66] (ILIT) can be a good complement to a CRT. In this scenario, you would create a second irrevocable trust alongside the CRT and fund it with the tax savings and part of the income from the CRT. The ILIT trustee could then purchase enough life insurance on the grantor's life to fully replace the assets funding the CRT, with the heirs as beneficiaries.

____

66   https://www.milvidlaw.com/taxes/benefits-of-a-charitable-remainder-trust/

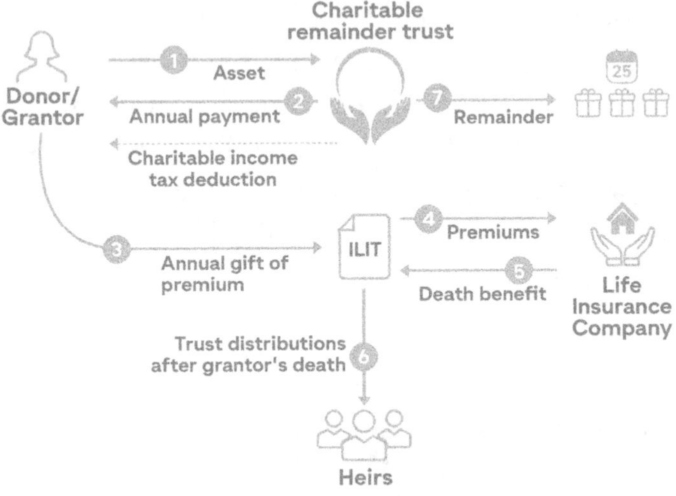

This works because life insurance is an inexpensive way to replace assets, with every dollar of premiums typically purchasing several dollars of insurance. Life insurance proceeds are paid out immediately on your death without getting bogged down in probate, but because they remain in the ILIT, you control the timing of the disposition of those funds through the trust document. Furthermore, these proceeds are paid out income-tax free, and because they are not considered part of your estate, they avoid estate taxes as well. Again, the idea here is to leverage tax savings to maximize wealth surplus that will be used to meet your legacy giving goals.

PRIVATE FOUNDATIONS

Up to this point, we have talked about several tools that can be used to maximize charitable giving. In general, I am a big advocate of Donor Advised Funds as an optimal vehicle for the vast majority of charitable legacy builders, given its relatively low cost, low administrative burden, and high charitable income tax deduction limits[67]. However, there are some ultra-high net worth charitable legacy builders for whom a private foundation might be a good option to consider, particularly for those who have amassed large amounts of wealth before turning their attention to charitable endeavors (because they typically have the ability to meet the larger initial funding requirements of foundations).

The major advantage proffered by a foundation[68] is the higher level of control it gives donors over the charitable giving process. A DAF is essentially an account held by a sponsoring charitable entity in the donor's name. The donor has advisory rights to give direction to the charitable giving process, but ultimately, the legal authority rests with the

[67] https://www.nptrust.org/donor-advised-funds/daf-vs-foundation/

[68] https://www.kiplinger.com/article/taxes/t055-c032-s014-choosing-private-foundation-or-donor-advised-fund.html

sponsoring entity. In contrast, a foundation is its own distinct legal entity controlled by the founder and a board of directors, and the foundation can hire family or board members as employees.

Some argue[69] this makes private foundations more conducive to bringing together a group of people, such as a family, around a common charitable goal. However, I would contend that as long as the DAF sponsoring entity allows the ability to name successor advisors (someone who receives advisory rights to the DAF in the event of your death), and many do, this provides the jumping off point to begin engaging children and grandchildren around the charitable vision and setting the expectation that the wealth stewardship and philanthropic responsibilities will eventually rest with them. Either way, though, if you want your charitable legacy to be sustainable through generations, it is critical to communicate openly and intentionally with family to ensure the charitable vision doesn't die with you. Best practices involve meeting regularly as a family, particularly at year-end, to review the various charitable organizations the family members are passionate about, and then allocating the charitable gifts accordingly.

---

69   https://www.501c3.org/private-foundation-vs-donor-advised-fund/

CHARITABLE ANNUITY AND POOLED INCOME FUNDS

For those who like the split-interest nature of a CRT, where you can benefit from a stream of income for life before passing assets on to charity, but are not crazy about the attorney fees and trustee fees of a CRT, a charitable gift annuity[70] (CGA) may be an option to consider. CGAs are offered by many large non-profits and involve signing a contract with the non-profit in which you give them a large donation, and in exchange they will send you fixed annual payments from the donation over your lifetime. At the end of your life (as well as your spouse's life, if it's a joint gift), the charity receives the remainder. You are then entitled to a charitable income tax deduction for the present value of the gift, and a portion of the annuity payments may be tax-free as well. Finally, you can gift appreciated property to get an extra tax benefit, as discussed in previous sections of this book.

Pooled income funds[71] are like CGAs, except you pool your donation with other donors, kind of like a charitable mutual fund, and receive income distributions from the fund based on your ownership

---

70 https://www.fidelitycharitable.org/guidance/philanthropy/charitable-gift-annuity.html

71 https://www.pgdc.com/pgdc/pooled-income-fund

share. After your death, the portion of the fund attributable to your ownership share is severed from the fund and used by the charity. Assets contributed to the fund receive an immediate charitable income tax deduction for the present value of the future charitable gift.

CONCLUSION

Hopefully you found this book to be helpful and informative along your journey to creating a lasting legacy of giving back. Again, this book just scratches the surface of the myriad considerations and nuances of legacy planning, and you will find more in-depth explorations of these topics in my blog, The Legacy Builder, which can be found at charislegacy.com/blog. Also, my firm, Charis Legacy Partners, is a wealth advisory firm specializing in legacy planning, and we would be happy to assist if you need additional hands-on help along the way. Godspeed to you in this journey, and may your legacy be great!